MW00630330

THE NĀMAKARAṆA
नामकरण

Naming of the Child

by
Āṅgirasa Muni

1999
Sacred Books, Inc.

First Printing March, 1999

Copyright © 1999
Aṅgiras Temple

This book is copyright under the Berne Convention. All rights are reserved. Apart from any fair dealing for the purpose of private study, research, criticism or review, as permitted under the Copyright Act, 1956, no part of this publication may be reproduced, stored in a retrieval system, or transmitted, in any form or by any means, electronic, electrical, chemical, mechanical, optical, photocopying, recording or otherwise, without the prior permission of the copyright owner. Inquiries should be addressed to the Publisher.

Publisher:
Sacred Books, Inc.
P. O. Box 11388
Fort Wayne, IN 46857-1388

ISBN 1-893152-09-X
The Library of Congress Catalog Card Number 98-090795

Composed by Devendra Agarwal, A-704, Sector C, Mahanagar, Lucknow, U.P., India
Printed in the United State of America

CONTENTS

Preface

This book forms part of the bigger book titled, The Gṛhyasūtra. The Author gratefully acknowledges the help of Mrs. Sunita Sharma in compiling the Names of Boys and Girls.

Āṅgirasa Muni

The Name Selection Process

Name is the most important piece of information a person gives to others about himself or herself; and yet he or she has no participation in deciding what his or her name will be. It is, therefore, a very important responsibility of the parents to name their child with due care. A name does affect the personality of the child as he grows. Parents can either give a child a good start or a bad start by the name they give their child.

Up until fifty years ago, many parents in India did not do a good job of naming their children. When you hear names such as Ghasīṭāmal, Bhikhārīmal, Munnī Lāl, Bābū Lāl, or Asharfī Devī, you wonder why these names found favor when hundreds of good names were waiting to be picked up.

Parents should select a name for their child which is (a) easy to pronounce; (2) which sounds good; and (3) which has a good meaning. If a name does not qualify on any of these counts it should be rejected. Parents should not select a name just because it sounds good. Do not name your daughter Anāmikā or Kinnarī, simply because the meanings of these words are not as flattering as their sounds are.

Many parents do not take enough care to find out the correct Saṃskṛta spelling of the name they choose. This is specially so when they firm up the English spelling of the name of their child. For example, they would spell the names as Shārdā instead of Shāradā, Ārtī instead of Āratī, and Nandnī instead of Nandinī. This is not fair to the child. Also there has been a tendency among Hindūs to abbreviate their name to the English initials. In so doing Krishnakānt Dās becomes K. K. Das. Some of them want to be called by their English initials such as KK, in this case. The Englishmen and the Americans do not do it. Why did your parents give you a name when you have no use for it? People should take pride in their name and not reduce it in this fashion. If you do not like your name for some reason you can legally change it.

Since there is no good way of spelling a Hindū name in English, Hindūs should start using diacritical marks when writing their names. This will remove any mistake of pronunciation. The list of names provided here contains these marks. We have purposely not followed the internationally accepted system of transliteration of Saṃskṛta into English. According to strict rules of Saṃskṛta many words should be spelled with an a at the end, for example, correct spelling is Nātha for नाथ but Nāth is acceptable. We have provided the English name-spellings that are considered convenient and desirable.

In many southern States of India there is a system of naming where the name of the village, the name of the father and the specific name of the child are made part of the name of the child in that order. For example Dēvanpallī Narahari Rāmaprakāsh. In this name Dēvanpallī is the name of the village, Narahari is the name of the father, and Rāmaprakāsh is the name of the child. There are many advantages in naming a child in this manner. It tells much more about the child than a name that is not organized in this fashion. It also obviates the need to proclaim the caste of the child which is an excellent thing. Separation of Hindūs into castes has been the one single most important reason for their downfall. Including the name of the father in the name is, more or less, a

Vedic tradition when the son of Kuśika had Kauśika as his last name. Yet, in keeping with modern and global times it is suggested that the specific name of the child be allowed to come first instead of last.

Finally, many Hindūs have started giving their child a foreign name such as Natāshā. While this action cannot be condemned, it is not highly recommended either. Why a foreign name? It is time that Hindūs feel proud of their own heritage and select a name among hundreds of beautiful Hindū names available.

THE NAMING CEREMONY
नामकरण संस्कार

The Appointment of the Priest — **पुरोहित नियुक्ति**

यावत् कर्म - समाप्तिस् तावत् ब्रह्मा भव।
आचार्यो भव वृतोऽस्मीति प्रतिवचनम्।।

yāvat karma samāptis tāvat brahmā bhava
ācāryō bhava vṛtō'smīti prativacanam

Father of Newborn — **नवजात का पिता**

Ācārya — आचार्य

I hereby appoint you purohita for the naming ceremony of my son/daughter

मैं आपको अपने पुत्र/पुत्री के नामकरण संस्कार का पुरोहित नियुक्त करता हूँ ।

> *Father of the newborn puts vertical tilaka on the forehead of the purōhita and a garland around his neck.*

Purōhita — **पुरोहित**

वृतोऽस्मि
vṛtō'smi

वृतोऽस्मि

I accept this appointment with pleasure.

आपका प्रस्ताव मुझे सहर्ष स्वीकार है ।

Svastivacana
(स्वस्तिवचन)

ॐ स्वस्ति न इन्द्रो वृद्धश्रवाः स्वस्ति नः पूषा विश्ववेदाः।
स्वस्ति नस् तार्क्ष्यो अरिष्टनेमिः स्वस्ति नो बृहस्पतिर् दधातु।।

|| ऋ. 1-89-6 ||

Ōṃ svasti na indrō vṛddhaśravāḥ svasti naḥ pūṣā viśvavēdāḥ
svasti nas tārkṣyō ariṣṭanēmiḥ svasti nō bṛhaspatir dadhātu

May Dēva Indra, the glorious, augment our welfare;
May Dēva Pūṣan, the all-knowing, augment our welfare;
May Dēva Sūrya, the protector from misfortunes, augment
our welfare;
May Dēva Bṛhaspati, the granter of wisdom, augment our
welfare.

Purification
पवित्रीकरण

Priest to put tilaka on the foreheads of the main participants and himself. Two persons to go around and put tilaka on guests. Priest to chant:

ॐ अपवित्रः पवित्रो वा सर्वावस्थां गतोऽपि वा।
यः स्मरेत् पुण्डरीकाक्षं स बाह्याभ्यन्तरः शुचिः।।

Ōm apavitraḥ pavitrō vā sarvāvasthāṃ gatō'pi vā
yaḥ smarēt puṇḍarīkākṣaṃ sa bāhyābhyantaraḥ śuciḥ

Lord, purify us inside and outside for participating in this ceremony

भगवन्! हमें मन, वचन, और शरीर से पवित्र करें ताकि हम यह समारोह प्रारम्भ कर सकें।

पुनन्तु मा देवजनाः पुनन्तु मनसा धियः।
पुनन्तु विश्वा भूतानि जातवेदः पुनीहि मा।।
।। य. 19-39 ।।

punantu mā dēvajanāḥ punantu manasā dhiyaḥ
punantu viśvā bhūtāni jātavēdaḥ punīhi mā

O Dēvas! please purify me; cleanse my heart and my mind. Cleanse my whole being. Cleanse the hearts of mankind.

Every one present to repeat after the purōhita, first in Saṃskṛta and then in English

Main Mantra

ॐ विश्वानि देव सवितर्	Ōṃ viśvāni dēva savitar
दुरितानि परासुव	duritāni parāsuva
यद् भद्रं	yad bhadraṃ
तन्न आसुव	tanna āsuva

O lord of the universe!
the stimulator of good thoughts.
We ask you to steer us away from the evil path.
Please put us on a course
which has your blessings.

श्री गणेशाय नमः	Śrī Gaṇēśāya namaḥ
ॐ ब्रह्मणे नमः	Ōṃ Brahmaṇē namaḥ
देविलक्ष्म्यै नमः	Dēvi Lakṣmyai namaḥ
देविसरस्वत्यै नमः	Dēvi Sarasvatyai namaḥ
देविदुर्गायै नमः	Dēvi Durgāyai namaḥ
ॐ शिवाय नमः	Ōṃ Śivāya namaḥ
श्री रामचन्द्राय नमः	Śrī Rāmacandrāya namaḥ
श्री केशवाय नमः	Śrī Kēśavāya namaḥ
ॐ विष्णवे नमः	Ōṃ Viṣṇavē namaḥ
सर्वेभ्यो देवेभ्यो नमः	sarvēbhyō Dēvēbhyō namaḥ

शान्ति मन्त्र

ॐ पृथिवी शान्तिरन्तरिक्षं शान्तिर्द्यौः
शान्तिरापः शान्तिरोषधयः शान्तिर्
वनस्पतयः शान्तिर् विश्वे मे देवाः शान्तिः
सर्वे मे देवाः शान्तिः शान्तिः शान्तिः शान्तिभिः ।
ताभिः शान्तिभिः सर्व शान्तिभिः
शमयामोऽहं यदिह घोरं यदिह क्रूरं
यदिह पापं तच्छान्तं तच्छिवं सर्वमेव शमस्तु नः ।।
।। अ. 19-9-14 ।।

Ōṃ pṛthivī śāntirantarikṣaṃ śāntirdyauḥ
śāntirāpaḥ śāntirōṣadhayaḥ śāntir
vanaspatayaḥ śāntir viśvē mē dēvāḥ śāntiḥ
sarvē mē dēvāḥ śāntiḥ śāntiḥ śāntiḥ śāntibhiḥ .
tābhiḥ śāntibhiḥ sarva śāntibhiḥ
śamayāmō'haṃ yadiha ghōraṃ yadiha krūraṃ
yadiha pāpaṃ tacchāntaṃ tacchivaṃ sarvamēva śamastu naḥ

Let us be in peace and harmony with our earth and with the skies.
Let us be in harmony with the waters and with the plant kingdom.
Let us be in harmony with the forests.
Let us be in peace and harmony with the Dēvas.
May we dedicate this invocation for harmony everywhere.
May the Lord make a gift of peace to us and to all men.
May harmony be established by removing what is dreadful.
May harmony be established by removing what is sinful.
Let peace and harmony reign everywhere.

Statement of Purpose

I, Ācārya ____________________ am the purōhita for the naming ceremony of the son/daughter of ____________________ and ________________________.

This ceremony will be performed on the basis of Āṅgirasa Gṛhyasūtra.

We are gathered here not only to witness the naming ceremony of the newborn and to congratulate the parents and grandparents for this blessed addition to their line but also to understand the significance of naming.

प्रयोजन का वक्तव्य

मैं आचार्य, ____________________ ____________________ और ____________________ के नवजात पुत्र/पुत्री के नामकरण संस्कार महोत्सव का पुरोहित हूँ।

यह संस्कार आङ्गिरस गृह्यसूत्र के अनुसार सम्पन्न किया जायेगा।

आज हम लोगों का यहाँ एकत्रित होने का प्रयोजन नामकरण का प्रत्यक्षदर्शी होना और माता पिता, दादा-दादी, नाना-नानी को बधाई देना ही नहीं अपितु यह भी विचार करना है कि उचित नामकरण कितना महत्त्व रखता है ।

Atha Saṅkalpa
(अथ सङ्कल्प)

ॐ विष्णुर् विष्णुर् विष्णुः

अद्यास्मिन् (1) ______________________
महाद्वीपे (2) ____________ देशे (3) ____________
राज्ये (4) ____________ नगरे (5) ____________ संवत्सरे
(6) ____________ मासे (7) ____________ शुभ पुण्य
तिथौ (8) ____________ वासरे (9) ____________ नामाहं
(10) ____________ नाम्नीं पत्नी सहितः
सकलदुरितोपशमनार्थं सर्वोपद्रव - विनाशहेतवे धर्मार्थ-काम-हेतवे ममात्मनो रोग-दोष-कष्ट-पीडा निवारणार्थम् अलक्ष्मी निवारणार्थं सपरिवारस्य मम क्षेमायुर् आरोग्यैश्वर्याभिवृद्ध्यर्थं तत्रादौ कार्य निर्विघ्नार्थं पूजनञ्च करिष्ये।

adyāsmin (1) ______________________
mahādvipē (2) ____________ dēśē (3) ____________
rājyē (4) ____________ nagarē (5) ____________
saṃvatsarē (6) ____________ māsē (7) ____________
śubha puṇya tithau (8) ____________ vāsarē (9) ____________
nāmāhaṃ (10) ____________ nāmnīṃ patnī sahitaḥ
sakala duritōpaśamanārthaṃ sarvōpadrava - vināśahētavē dharmārtha-kāma-hētavē mamātmanō rōga-dōṣa-kaṣṭa-pīḍā nivāraṇārtham alakṣmī nivāraṇārthaṃ saparivārasya mama kṣēmāyur ārōgyaiśvaryabhivṛddhyarthaṃ tatrādau kāryarnirvighnārthaṃ pūjanañca kariṣyē.

---

(1) n. of continent; (2) n. of country; (3) n. of State or Province; (4) n. of city; (5) year; (6) month; (7) date; (8) day; (9) name of the male worshipper. (10) name of the female worshipper.

Bring agnikuṇḍa with fire in it.

अग्निमीळे पुरोहितं यज्ञस्य देवम् ऋत्विजम्।
होतारं रत्नधातमम् ।। ।। ऋ. 1-1-1 ।।

agnimīḷē purōhitaṃ yajñasya dēvam ṛtvijam
hōtāraṃ ratnadhātamam

I glorify Agni, the divine priest and the messenger of my oblations to God who is the bestower of prosperity.

ॐ अग्नये स्वाहा । इदम् अग्नये इदं न मम ।।
ॐ प्रजापतये स्वाहा । इदं प्रजापतये, इदं न मम ।।
ॐ इन्द्राय स्वाहा । इदम् इन्द्राय, इदं न मम ।।

Ōm agnayē svāhā idam agnayē idaṃ na mama
Ōm prajāpatayē svāhā idaṃ prajāpatayē, idaṃ na mama
Ōm indrāya svāhā idam indrāya, idaṃ na mama

Every one present to recite the Gāyatrī mantrā three times

ॐ भूर् भुवः स्वः
तत् सवितुर् वरेण्यं
भर्गो देवस्य धीमहि
धियो यो नः प्रचोदयात् स्वाहा ।। ।। ऋ. 3-62-10 ।।

Ōṃ bhūr bhuvaḥ svaḥ
tat savitur varēṇyaṃ
bhargō dēvasya dhīmahi
dhiyō yō naḥ pracōdayāt svāhā

(The Earth, the Sky, and the Heaven praise Him.) Let us meditate on the glory of the divine Lord. He is the one who sustains us. We pray to Him that He may direct our understanding by instilling wisdom in us.

Commentary

This is the most famous of all vedic mantras, and is called Gāyatrī mantra after the meter in which it is composed. "Ōṃ bhūr, bhuvaḥ, svaḥ" are not part of the mantra. Ōṃ is always put at the beginning of the utterance of one or a set of mantras. "Bhūr, bhuvaḥ, svaḥ", the set of three words is called vyāhṛti. It is always added to this mantra and also to many other mantras.

ॐ स्वस्ति पन्थामनुचरेम सूर्याचन्द्रमसाविव।
पुनर् ददताघ्नता जानता सं गमेमहि।।
।। ऋ. 5-51-15 ।।

Ōṃ svasti panthāmanucarēma sūryācandramasāviva
punar dadatāghnatā jānatā saṃ gamēmahi

Lord, we shall follow the virtuous path steadfastly like the sun and the moon follow their paths. We shall associate with the generous, the kind, and the learned.

ॐ कर्मसमृद्धिर् अस्तु - स्वाहा

Ōṃ karmasamṛddhir astu - svāhā

ॐ देवानां भद्रा सुमतिर् ऋजूयतां
देवानां रातिर् अभि नो नि वर्तताम् ।
देवानां सख्यमुप सेदिमा वयं
देवा न आयुः प्र तिरन्तु जीवसे ।।
।। ऋ. 1-89-2 ।।

Ōṃ dēvānāṃ bhadrā sumatir ṛjūyatāṃ
dēvānāṃ rātir abhi nō ni vartatām
dēvānāṃ sakhyamupa sēdimā vayaṃ
dēvā na āyuḥ pra tirantu jīvasē

O Dēvas! Shower your benevolence upon us. May you be generous to us ever, approving of the righteous among us. May we obtain your friendship; and may you grant us long life.

ॐ प्रजापते न त्वदेतान्यन्यो विश्वा जातानि परि ता बभूव।
यत् कामास् ते जुहुमस् तन् नो अस्तु वयं स्याम पतयो रयीणाम्।।
।। ऋ. 10-121-10 ।।

Ōṃ prajāpatē na tvadētānyanyō viśvā jātāni pari tā babhūva
yatkāmās tē juhumas tan nō astu vayaṃ syāma patayō rayīṇām

O Lord of all! None except you pervade everything and every being. May our wishes, for which we have come to pray you, be granted, May we become happy and prosperous.

The child should be taken in the lap by the mother, father, dādī, dādā, nānī and nānā in this sequence and each person should repeat the following and put sandalwood paste tilak on their forehead.

.... त्वमायुष्मान्, वर्चस्वी, तेजस्वी, श्रीमान्, भूयाः

.... tvamāyuṣmān, varcasvī, tējasvī, śrīmān, bhūyāḥ

O Newborn!
I am your ....
On this day, I name you ....

May you live long and attain glory.

हे नवजात!
मै तेरा/तेरी .... हूँ।
मै तुझे .... नाम
से सुशोभित करता/करती हूँ

भगवान् से प्रार्थना है कि तू दीर्घजीवी और तेजस्वी हो ।

Put tilaka on the forehead of the child

ॐ तच् चक्षुर् देवहितं पुरस्ताच् छुक्रम् उच्चरत्।
पश्येम शरदः शतं, जीवेम शरदः शतꣳ
शृणुयाम शरदः शतं, प्रब्रवाम शरदः शतम्,
अदीनाः स्याम शरदः शतं, भूयश्च शरदः शतात्।
॥ य. 36-24 ॥

Ōṃ tac cakṣur dēvahitaṃ purastāc chukram uccarat
paśyēma śaradaḥ śataṃ, jīvēma śaradaḥ śatam
śṛṇuyāma śaradaḥ śataṃ, prabravāma śaradaḥ śatam,
adīnāḥ syāma śaradaḥ śataṃ, bhūyaśca śaradaḥ śatāt

May we see "The Bright Eye" (The sunrise) for a hundred years.

May we be granted
- a hundred years to live;
- a hundrend years to see well;
- a hundred years to hear well;
- a hundred years to speak clearly;
- a hundred years of self-dependence;

Yes, all of the above, and even in excess of hundred years.

The following should be performed by parents and grand-parents. The performers should take water each time in their right palm and sip it after each svāhā

ॐ अमृतोपस्तरणम् असि स्वाहा।
ॐ अमृतापिधानम् असि स्वाहा।
ॐ सत्यं, यशः श्रीर् मयि श्रीः श्रयन्ताम् स्वाहा।

Ōm amṛtōpastaraṇam asi svāhā
Ōm amṛtāpidhānam asi svāhā
Ōṃ satyaṃ, yaśaḥ śrīr mayi śrīḥ śrayantām svāhā

May this water bring happy life to ....*
May the Immortal One Support ....*
May ....* attain glory, honor, and prosperity in life by following the path of truth.

* newborn's name

ॐ नमः शम्भवाय च
मयोभवाय च
नमः शंकराय च
मयस्कराय च
नमः शिवाय च
शिवतराय च ।। स्वाहा ।। ।। य. 16-41 ।।

Ōṃ namaḥ śambhavāya ca
mayōbhavāya ca
namaḥ śaṃkarāya ca
mayaskarāya ca
namaḥ śivāya ca
śivatarāya ca svāhā

Salutations to you O God!
the granter of welfare,
the source of happiness.
the beneficent
the cause of joy
the auspicious,
the source of greatest bliss

Recite the following āhuti 3 times putting sāmagrī oblation in the fire.

ॐ सर्वं वै पूर्णꣳ स्वाहा
Ōṃ sarvaṃ vai pūrṇaṃ svāhā

आरती जय जगदीश हरे
Āratī jaya jagadīśa harē

English Spellings of Hindū Names

Even though there is a standard, internationally approved, system of transliteration of Saṃskṛta words into Roman (English) script this system cannot be used completely for spelling the names. In spelling Hindū names substantial compromise takes place even though this compromise, in strict sense, results in erroneous spelling.

The most outstanding deviation from true transliteration lies in omitting 'a' from the end in most words, for example Rāma (राम) is written as Rām and Amita (अमित) is written Amit. Yet whenever two consonants come together at the end the 'a' is not omitted, for example Krishna is not written Krishn. Also we recommend that ya (य) sound as in Vijaya be not abbreviated to Vijay because the latter is likely to be pronounced by the uninformed as VJ.

Compromises

आ	ā	written as	a	ञ	ña	written as	na
ई	ī	written as	i	ट्	ṭ	written as	t
ऊ	ū	written as	u	ठ्	ṭh	written as	th
ऋ	ṛ	written as	ri	ड्	ḍ	written as	d
ङ	ṅa	written as	na	ढ्	ḍh	written as	dh
च	ca	written as	ch	ण्	ṇ	written as	n
छ	cha	written as	chha	श्	ś	written as	sh
				ष्	ṣ	written as	sh

Note that these compromises are costly; for example बुद्ध and बुड्ढा are written identically as a result of the compromises.

Names for Boys

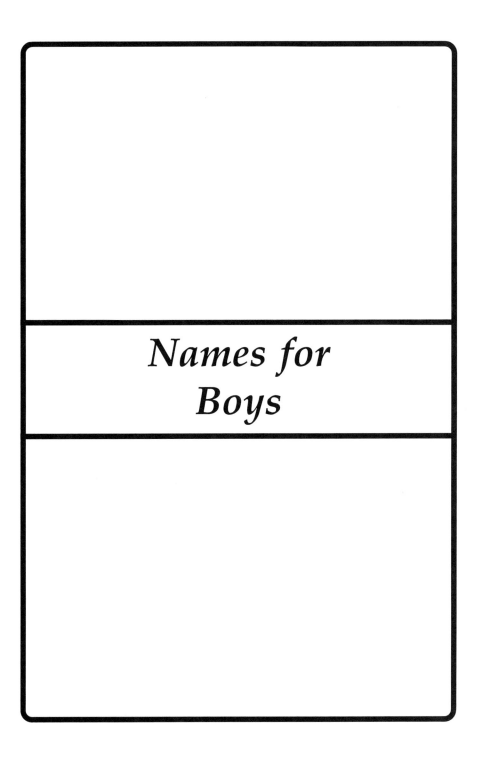

Recommended First Names for Boys

अंशुमान्	Aṃśumān - the sun
अंशुल	Aṃśula - radiant, e. of Cāṇakya
अंसल	Aṃsala - strong
अक्षत	Akṣata - unbroken. unblemished
अक्षय	Akṣaya - Imperishable
अखिल	Akhila - complete, whole
अखिलेश	Akhilēśa - lord of the Universe
अगस्त्य	Agastya - n. of a ṛṣi, n. of a star
अङ्कुर	Aṅkura - sprout
अङ्गद्	Aṅgad - n. of the son of Bālī
अच्युत	Acyuta - e. of Śrī Kṛṣṇa meaning infallible
अजय	Ajaya - unconquered, invincible
अजित	Ajita - undefeatable
अजिताभ	Ajitābha - undefeatable and radiant
अजेय	Ajēya - undefeatable
अतुल्य	Atulya - matchless
अतुल्यतेज	Atulyatēja - matchless radiance
अत्रि	Atri - n. of a ṛṣi
अधीश	Adhīśa - lord
अनघ	Anagha - sinless
अनन्त	Ananta - endless, e. of serpent Śeśa
अनादि	Anādi - having no beginning
अनिरुद्ध	Aniruddha - self-willed, n. of the grandson of Śrī Kṛṣṇa
अनुकूल	Anukūla - favorable
अनुरुद्ध	Anuruddha - pacified
अनमोल	Anamōla - priceless (Hindī)
अपार	Apāra - boundless
अपूर्व	Apūrva - unprecedented
अभय	Abhaya - fearless
अभिजित	Abhijita - victorious
अभिनव	Abhinava - quite new

अभिषेक	Abhiṣēka - anointing
अभ्युदय	Abhyudaya - rise, elevation
अमर	Amara - immortal
अमरदीप	Amaradīpa - eternal lamp
अमित	Amita - without measure
अमिताभ	Amitābha - immeasurable splendor
अमितायुष	Amitāyuṣa - immortal
अमृत	Amṛta - immortal, nectar, ambrosia
अमोघ	Amōgha - unerring
अम्बिका प्रसाद	Ambikā Prasāda - the grace of Goddess Durgā
अम्बुज	Ambuja - lotus
अयोध्यानाथ	Ayōdhyānātha - e. of Srī Rāma
अरविन्द	Aravinda - lotus
अरित्र	Aritra - propeller of boat
अरुज	Aruja - healthy
अरुण	Aruṇa - red, the dawn
अर्चित	Arcita - worshipped
अर्जुन	Arjuna - pure, white
अर्हत	Arhata - worthy, revered
अलङ्कार	Alaṅkāra - ornament
अवनीश	Avanīśa - the lord of the earth
अवनीन्द्र	Avanīndra- the lord of the earth
अवलोकितेश्वर	Avalōkitēśvara - n. of a Bōdhisattva
अविचल	Avicala - firm
अविनाश	Avināśa - imperishable
अशेष	Aśēṣa - perfect
अशोक	Aśōka - without sorrow
अश्विन्	Aśvin - n. of two divine physicians
असित	Asita - n. of a ṛṣi
असीम	Asīma - unlimited
आकाश	Ākāśa - sky
आकाशदीप	Ākāśadīpa - a lamp lighted in honor of Viṣṇu
आत्मानन्द	Ātmānanda - the rejoicing spirit

आदर्श	Ādarśa - ideal
आदित्य	Āditya - s. of Aditi, sun
आदीप	Ādīpa - to illuminate
आनन्द	Ānanda - delight
आनन्दप्रकाश	Ānandaprakāśa - expression of delight
आनन्दस्वरूप	Ānandasvarūpa - very image of joy
आमोद	Āmōda - joy
आराधन	Ārādhana - worship
आरोही	Ārōhī - elevating
आलोक	Ālōka - light
आशीष	Āśīṣa - blessing
आशु	Āśu - fast
आशुतोष	Āśutōṣa - easily pleased
आह्लाद	Āhlāda - happiness
इन्दीवर	Indīvara - blue lotus
इन्दु	Indu - moon
इन्दुकमल	Indukamala - the moon
इन्दुकान्त	Indukānta - moonstone
इन्दुमणि	Indumaṇi - moonstone
इन्दुमुख	Indumukha - face beautiful as moon
इन्दुरत्न	Induratna - pearl
इन्दुशेखर	Induśēkhara - e. of Śiva
इन्द्र	Indra - n. of a divinity
इन्द्रगुप्त	Indragupta - protected by Indra
इन्द्रतेज	Indratēja - Indra's radiance
इन्द्रदत्त	Indradatta - gift of Indra
इन्द्रनील	Indranīla - sapphire
इन्द्रसेन	Indrasēna - n. of the s. of Yudhiṣṭhira
इन्द्राभ	Indrābha - Indra's splendor
ईशान	Īśāna - wealthy, a king
ईश्वरचन्द्र	Īśvaracandra - n. of a k.
ईश्वरदयालु	Īśvaradayālu - one blessed by God
ईश्वरप्रसाद	Īśvaraprasāda - God's grace

उग्रसेन	Ugrasēna - aggressive army leader
उज्ज्वल	Ujjvala - shining, clean
उत्कर्ष	Utkarṣa - elevation, growth
उत्तम	Uttama - excellent
उत्पल	Utpala - blossoming of the blue lotus
उत्साह	Utsāha - enthusiasm
उदज	Udaja - lotus
उदय	Udaya - appearance, elevation
उदयन	Udayana - rise, result
उदयी	Udayī - rising, prosperous
उदित	Udita - risen
उद्दीप	Uddīpa - radiant
उद्भास	Udbhāsa - splendor
उद्यम	Udyama - diligence
उपमन्यु	Upamanyu - striving
उमाकान्त	Umākānta - Śiva, the consort of Umā
उमेश	Umēśa - Śiva, the husband of Umā
उर्वीश	Urvīśa - king
उल्लास	Ullāsa - mirth
ऊर्जित	Ūrjita - energetic
ऋजु	Ṛju - simple
ऋतम्भर	Ṛtambhara - of true nature
ऋतुपर्ण	Ṛtuparṇa - guardian of divine truths
ऋतुराज	Ṛturāja - spring, the king of seasons
ऋभु	Ṛbhu - skillful
ऋषभ	Ṛṣabha - excellent
ऋषि	Ṛṣi - seer, contributor to the Vēdas
ऐश्वर्य	Aiśvarya - supremacy
ओम्	Ōm - the Sacred syllable
ओम्कार	Ōṃkāra - (same as Ōm)
ओम्प्रकाश	Ōṃprakāśa - the radiance of Ōm
कनिष्क	Kaniṣka - n. of a king
कपिल	Kapila - the sun

कमल	Kamala - lotus
कमलनयन	Kamalanayana - lotus-eyed
कमलापति	Kamalāpati - e. of Viṣṇu
कमलेश	Kamalēśa - e. of Viṣṇu
कल्याण	Kalyāṇa - welfare, n. of a rāga
कवि	Kavi - intelligent, poet
कवीन्दु	Kavīndu - outstandingly intelligent
कार्त्तिक	Kārttika - (short of Kārttikēya)
कार्त्तिकेय	Kārttikēya - n. of a son of Śiva
काशीनाथ	Kāśīnātha - e. of Śiva
किरण	Kiraṇa - ray of light
कुलदीप	Kuladīpa - glory of the family
कुलभूषण	Kulabhūṣaṇa - ornament of the family
कुश	Kuśa - n. of the eldest son of Śrī Rāma
कुशल	Kuśala - competent
कुसुमाकर	Kusumākara - treasure of flowers
कृष्णकान्त	Kṛṣṇakānta - the handsome Śrī Kṛṣṇa
कृष्ण चन्द्र	Kṛṣṇa Candra - the moon-faced Śrī Kṛṣṇa
कृष्ण दत्त	Kṛṣṇa Datta - gift of Śrī Kṛṣṇa
कृष्ण दयाल	Kṛṣṇa Dayāla - merciful Śrī Kṛṣṇa
कृष्ण दास	Kṛṣṇa Dāsa - the servant of Śrī Kṛṣṇa
कृष्ण प्रसाद	Kṛṣṇa Prasāda - the grace of Śrī Kṛṣṇa
कृष्ण मूर्ति	Kṛṣṇa Mūrti - the form of Śrī Kṛṣṇa
केतन	Kētana - abode
केदार नाथ	Kēdāra Nātha - e. of Śiva
केशव	Kēśava - e. of Śrī Kṛṣṇa
कैलास चन्द्र	Kailāsa Candra - e. of Śiva
कैलास नाथ	Kailāsa Nātha - e. of Śiva
कौशल	Kauśala - skillfulness
क्षेत्रपाल	Kṣētrapāla - e. of Śiva
गगन चन्द्र	Gagana Candra - moon in the sky
गङ्गाधर	Gaṅgādhara - e. of Śiva
गणपति	Gaṇapati - the Lord of beings

गणेश	Gaṇēśa - the Lord of beings
गिरिजा प्रसाद	Girijā Prasāda - the grace of Durgā
गिरीश	Girīśa - e. of Śiva
गोपाल	Gōpāla - cowherd - e. of Śrī Kṛṣṇa
गोपेश	Gōpēśa - e. of Śrī Kṛṣṇa
गोविन्द	Gōvinda - e. of Śrī Kṛṣṇa
गौतम	Gautama - n. of Buddha
गौरव	Gaurava - glory
गौरीनाथ	Gaurīnātha - e. of Śiva
घनश्याम	Ghanaśyāma - e. of Śrī Kṛṣṇa
चतुर्भुज	Caturbhuja - e. of Viṣṇu of four arms
चन्द्रकान्त	Candrakānta - beautiful moon
चन्द्रकेतु	Candrakētu - bright moon
चन्द्रगुप्त	Candragupta - protected by moon
चन्द्रदत्त	Candradatta - the gift of moon
चन्द्रप्रकाश	Candraprakāśa - the radiance of moon
चन्द्र भूषण	Candra Bhūṣaṇa - e. of Śiva
चन्द्रमुख	Candramukha - moon-faced
चन्द्रशेखर	Candraśēkhara - e. of Śiva
चन्द्रानन	Candrānana - moon-faced
चन्द्र भास	Candra Bhāsa - moon-like
चारु दत्त	Cāru Datta - the beautiful gift
चित्ररथ	Citraratha - owner of a bright chariot
चिदानन्द	Cidānanda - indeed blissful
चिन्तामणि	Cintāmaṇi - wish-yielding gem
चेतन	Cētana - soul, intelligence
चैतन्य	Caitanya - consciousness
च्यवन	Cyavana - active, n. of a ṛṣi
छत्रपति	Chatrapati - king
छत्रसाल	Chatrasāla - n. of a prince
जगजीवन	Jagajīvana - God, giver of life
जगत् प्रकाश	Jagat Prakāśa - the light of the world
जगदीश	Jagadīśa - lord of the world

जगन्नाथ	Jagannātha - lord of the world, e. of Viṣṇu or Śrī Kṛṣṇā
जगमोहन	Jagamōhana - one who entices everyone
जनार्‌दन	Janārdana - e. of Śrī Kṛṣṇa - destroyer of the wicked
जमदग्‌नि	Jamadagni - n. of a ṛṣi
जयकृष्ण	Jayakṛṣṇa - glory to Śrī Kṛṣṇa
जयराम	Jayarāma - glory to Śrī Rāma
जयन्त	Jayanta - Victorious
जानकीनाथ	Jānakīnātha - e. of Śrī Rāma
जितेन्‌द्रिय	Jitēndriya - master of senses
जीवन कृष्ण	Jīvana Kṛṣṇa - Śrī Kṛṣṇa - our very life
ज्ञान प्रकाश	Jñāna Prakāśa - the light of knowledge
ज्ञानेन्द्र/ज्ञानेश	Jñānēndra/Jñānēśa - the lord of knowledge
ज्योतिर्‌मय	Jyōtirmaya - brilliant
तपन	Tapana - radiant, sun
तारानाथ	Tārānātha - e. of Śivā
तिलक	Tilaka - sacred mark on the forehead
तुषारगिरि	Tuṣāragiri - snow-capped mountain
तेजसिंह	Tējasiṃha - the splendor of a lion
तेजस	Tējasa - majesty
त्रिलोक नाथ	Trilōka Nātha - the lord of three worlds
त्रिलोकी नाथ	Trilōkī Nātha - e. of Viṣṇu
त्रिलोचन नाथ	Trilōcana Nātha - e. of Śiva
त्र्यम्बक नाथ	Tryambaka Nātha - father of three worlds - e. of Śiva
दशरथ	Daśaratha - n. of the father of Śrī Rāma
दामोदर	Dāmōdara - e. of Śrī Kṛṣṇa
दिनेश	Dinēśa - sun
दिलीप	Dilīpa - n. of an ancestor of Śrī Rāma
दिवाकर	Divākara - sun
दीपक	Dīpaka - lamp
दीपङ्कर	Dīpaṅkara - the cause of light, n. of a Buddha
दुर्‌गादत्त	Durgādatta - gift of Durgā
दुर्‌गा प्रसाद	Durgā Prasāda - grace of Durgā
दुष्यन्त	Duṣyanta - n. of the king who was father of Bharata

देव दत्त Dēva Datta - gift of angels
देव दास Dēva Dāsa - devotee of God
देवानन्द Dēvānanda - delighter of gods
देवाशिष Dēvāśiṣa - the blessing of gods
देवेन्द्र Dēvēndra - Indra
देवेश Dēvēśa - the chief of Dēvas
द्वारका नाथ Dvārakā Nātha - e. of Śrī Kṛṣṇa
धनञ्जय Dhanañjaya - victor over materialism, e. of Arjuna
धन्वन्तरि Dhanvantari - rainbow colored boat, n. of the founder of Hindū school of medicine
धर्मनेत्र Dharmanētra - n. of a ṛsi
धर्मराज Dharmarāja - just king, e. of K. Yudhiṣṭhira
धर्मेन्द्र/धर्मेश Dharmēndra/Dharmēśa - just and fair king
धीरेन्द्र/धीरेश Dhīrēndra/Dhīrēśa - patient king or master
ध्रुव Dhruva - permanent, eternal
नकुल Nakula - brown complexioned, n. of a Pāṇḍava prince
नगेन्द्र Nagēndra - lord of mountains, e. of Himālaya
नन्दन Nandana - delighter of people, son
नमित Namita - modest
नरेन्द्र/नरेश Narēndra/Narēśa - king of men
नरोत्तम Narōttama - best among men
नलिन Nalina - lotus
नवीन Navīna - new, modern
नवीन चन्द्र Navīna Candra - new moon
नवेन्दु Navēndu - new moon
नारायण Nārāyaṇa - another n. of Viṣṇu
निखिल Nikhila - whole, complete, entire
निखिलेश Nikhilēśa - lord of all - God
निरञ्जन Nirañjana - pure
निर्मल Nirmala - clean
निर्मल चन्द्र Nirmala Candra - pure moon
निलय Nilaya - home
नीरज Nīraja - lotus

नीरद	Nīrada - cloud
नीरव	Nīrava - quiet
नील	Nīla - blue, dark
नीलमणि	Nīlamaṇi - sapphire
नीलकण्ठ	Nīlakaṇṭha - peacock, blue-throated - e. of Śiva
पङ्कज	Paṅkaja - lotus
परमानन्द	Paramānanda - supreme felicity
परमेश्वर	Paramēśvara - Supreme Lord
- दयाल	- Dayāla - merciful God
- दास	- Dāsa - servant of God
- नाथ	- Nātha - Supreme Lord and Master
- प्रसाद	- Prasāda - grace of God
पराग	Parāga - pollen of flower
परितोष	Paritōṣa - satisfied
परिमल	Parimala - fragrance
परिक्षित्	Parikṣit - n. of a Pāṇḍava king who was the grandson of Arjuna
पवन	Pavana - wind
पारिजात	Pārijāta - fragrance, n. of a tree of paradise
पार्थ	Pārtha - son of Pṛthā - e. of Arjuna
पार्थसारथि	Pārthasārathi - charioteer of Arjuna - e. of Śrī Kṛṣṇa
पीयूष	Pīyūṣa - nectar
पुनीत	Punīta - clean, sacred
पुरारि	Purāri - e. of Śiva
पुरुषोत्तम	Puruṣōttama - Supreme Soul, best of men
पुष्कर	Puṣkara - blue lotus, n. of a place of pilgrimage
पुष्करनाथ	Puṣkaranātha - God
पूर्ण चन्द्र	Pūrṇa Candra - full moon
प्रकाश चन्द्र	Prakāśa Candra - moon-light
प्रणव	Praṇava - sacred syllable Ōm
प्रताप	Pratāpa - glory, influence
प्रत्यूष	Pratyūṣa - dawn, sun
प्रदीप	Pradīpa - light, lamp

प्रद्युम्न	Pradyumna - mighty
प्रफुल्ल	Praphulla - cheerful, blooming
प्रबोध	Prabōdha - wise, awakened
प्रबोध चन्द्र	Prabōdha Candra - wise and radiant
प्रभाकर	Prabhākara - sun, moon
प्रभात	Prabhāta - dawn
प्रभु दयाल	Prabhu Dayāla - merciful lord
प्रमोद	Pramōda - happy
प्रवीण	Pravīṇa - dexterous
प्रवीर	Pravīra - mighty, chief, hero
प्रशान्त	Praśānta - calm, composed
प्रसन्न	Prasanna - pleased
प्रसाद	Prasāda - grace, gift, blessing
प्रसून	Prasūna - flower
प्रांशु	prāṃśu - tall, strong
प्राञ्जल	prāñjala - straight, honest
प्रियदर्शन	Priyadarśana - good-looking
प्रियदर्शी	Priyadarśī - handsome
प्रियव्रत	Priyavrata - of good character
प्रेम	Prēma - love, affection
- चन्द्र	- Candra - love and brightness
- दत्त	- Datta - gift of love
- दयाल	- Dayāla - kind and loving
- नाथ	- Nātha - loving master
- प्रकाश	- Prakāśa - expression of love
- प्रताप	- Pratāpa - power of love
- सागर	- Sāgara - ocean of love
बलदेव/बलभद्र	Baladēva/Balabhadra - n. of the elder brother of Śrī Kṛṣṇa
बलराम	Balarāma - (see Baladēva)
बालकृष्ण	Bālakṛṣṇa - boy Kṛṣṇa
बालचन्द्र/बालेन्दु	Bālacandra/bālēndu - new moon
बृहस्पति	Bṛhaspati - the great master, original of Gaṇapati

बृहद्रथ	Bṛhadratha - n. of a king
ब्रह्मदत्त	Brahmadatta - gift of God
ब्रह्मप्रकाश	Brahmaprakāśa - light of God
ब्रह्मानन्द	Brahmānanda - the absolute bliss
भरत	Bharata - (n. of many famous persons)
भरद्वाज	Bharadvāja - n. of a ṛṣi
भवानी प्रसाद	Bhavānī Prasāda - grace of goddess Durgā
भारत	Bhārata - descendant of K. Bharat, n. of country
भास्कर	Bhāskara - sun
भुवन चन्द्र	Bhuvana Candra - earth and moon
भुवनेश	Bhuvanēśa - lord of the earth
भुवनेश्वर	Bhuvanēśvara - lord of the earth
भूपेन्द्र	Bhūpēndra - lord of the world
भूषण	Bhūṣaṇa - ornament
मकरन्द	Makaranda - honey
मङ्गल	Maṅgala - welfare
मञ्जुल	Mañjula - handsome, charming
मदनकृष्ण	Madana Kṛṣṇa - handsome Kṛṣṇa
मदन गोपाल	Madana Gōpāla - handsome Kṛṣṇa
मदन मोहन	Madana Mōhana - handsome Kṛṣṇa
मधु	Madhu - honey
मधुर	Madhura - sweet, charming
मधुसूदन	Madhusūdana - e. of Kṛṣṇa
मनमोहन	Manamōhana - e. of Kṛṣṇa
मनीषी	Manīṣī - intelligent, wise
मनु	Manu - n. of the first man
मनोज	Manōja - charming, e. of Cupid
मनोहर	Manōhara - attractive, handsome
मन्मथ नाथ	Manmatha Nātha - e. of Kāmadēva
मयङ्क	Mayaṅka - moon
महावीर	Mahāvīra - very brave
महेश	Mahēśa - great Lord, e. of Śiva
महेशचन्द्र	Mahēśacandra - the effulgent Lord Śiva

महेश दत्त	Mahēśa Datta - the gift of Śiva
महेश प्रसाद	Mahēśa Prasāda - the grace of Śiva
महेश्वर	Mahēśvara - great Lord, e. of Śiva
माधव	Mādhava - e. of Śrī Kṛṣṇa
मानस	Mānasa - mind
मिलिन्द	Milinda - bumble-bee
मिहिर	Mihira - sun
मुकुन्द	Mukunda - treasure, jewel, e. of Viṣṇu
मुकुल	Mukula - bud, soul
मुनीन्द्र	Munīndra - e. of Gautama Buddha
मुनीश	Munīśa - Chief among munis
मुरलीधर	Muralīdhara - the flute-player, e. of Śrī Kṛṣṇa
मुरारि	Murāri - enemy of Mura, e. of Śrī Kṛṣṇa
मृदुल	Mṛdula - tender
मेधावी	Mēdhāvī - brilliant
मोहित	Mōhita - attracted
मोहन	Mōhana - attractive
यतीन्द्र/यतीश	Yatīndra/Yatīśa - best among ascetics
यतेन्द्र	Yatēndra - (short form of Yatīndriya), meaning pure
यदुनाथ	Yadunātha - e. of Śrī Kṛṣṇa
यश	Yaśa - honor, fame
यशपाल	Yaśapāla - protector of fame
युधिष्ठिर	Yudhiṣṭhira - firm in battle
योगेन्द्र/योगेश/ योगेश्वर	Yōgēndra/Yōgēśa/Yōgēśvara - master of Yōga
रघुनन्दन	Raghunandana - e. of Srī Ramā
रघुनाथ/रघुपति/ रघुराज	Raghunātha/Raghupati/Raghurāja - the Lord among Raghus
रजत	Rajata - silver
रजनीकान्त	Rajanīkānta - the lord of night-moon
रजनीश	Rajanīśa - the lord of night-moon
रणजीत	Raṇajīta - victorious in war
रणवीर	Raṇavīra - brave warrior

रमण	Ramaṇa - handsome
रमाकान्त/	Ramākānta/
रमानाथ/	Ramānātha/
रमानिवास/रमेश	Ramānivāsa/Ramēśa - husband of Ramā - e. of Viṣṇu
रवि	Ravi - sun
रविकान्त	Ravikānta - splendor of sun
रविकिरण	Ravikiraṇa - ray of sun
रवीन्द्र	Ravīndra - sun and Indra
रसिक	Rasika - interested in pleasures, elegant
राकेश	Rākēśa - full moon, e. of Śiva
राघव	Rāghava - e. of Śrī Rāma
राघवेन्द्र	Rāghavēndra - e. of Śrī Rāma
राज कुमार	Rāja Kumāra - prince
राजा राम	Rājā Rāma - K. Rāma
राजेन्द्र/राजेश/ राजेश्वर	Rājēndra/Rājēśa/Rājēśvara - sovereign
राम	Rāma - attractive, n. of the human incarnation of God
राम किशोर/ राम कुमार	Rāma Kiśōra/Rāma Kumāra - young Śrī Rāma
रामकृष्ण/	Rāmakṛṣṇa/
रामगोपाल/	Rāmagōpāla/
रामगोविन्द	Rāmagōvinda - Śrī Rāma and Śrī Kṛṣṇa
रामचन्द्र	Rāmacandra - full name of Śrī Rāma
राम दत्त	Rāma Datta - gift of Śrī Rāma
राम दास	Rāma Dāsa - servant of Śrī Rāma
राम नाथ	Rāma Nātha - Lord Śrī Rāma
राम प्रसाद	Rāma Prasāda - grace of Śrī Rāma
राम प्रकाश	Rāma Prakāśa - glory of Śrī Rāma
राममूर्ति	Rāmamūrti - the image of Śrī Rāma
राममोहन	Rāmamōhana - charming Śrī Rāma
रामानन्द	Rāmānanda - Rāma, the delighter
रामानुज	Rāmānuja - younger brother of Śrī Rāma
रामेश्वर	Rāmēśvara - Lord Śrī Rāma

राहुल	Rāhula - n. of the s. of Gautama Buddha
रेवतीरमण	Rēvatīramaṇa - husband of Revatī - e. of Balarāma
रोहित	Rōhita - red, sun
लक्ष्मण	Lakṣmaṇa - auspicious, n. of a younger brother of Śrī Rāma
लक्ष्मीकान्त	Lakṣmīkānta - husband of Lakṣmī - e. of Viṣṇu
लक्ष्मीदत्त	Lakṣmīdatta - gift of Lakṣmī
ललित	Lalita - charming
ललित चन्द्र	Lalita candra - charming moon
ललित मोहन	Lalita mōhana - handsome Śrī Kṛṣṇa
ललितादित्य	Lalitāditya - beautiful sun
लोकनाथ/ लोकेन्द्र/लोकेश	Lōkanātha/ Lōkēndra/Lōkēśa - lord of the earth
वसन्त	Vasanta - spring season
वसिष्ठ	Vasiṣṭha - excellent, n. of a ṛṣi
वसुदेव	Vasudēva - good lord, n. of f. of Śrī Kṛṣṇa
वागीश/वागीश्वर	Vāgīśa/Vāgīśvara - the lord of speech - e. of Gaṇapati
वाचस्पति	Vācaspati - the lord of speech - e. of Gaṇapati
वामदेव	Vāmadēva - n. of a ṛṣi
वासुदेव	Vāsudēva - s. of Vasudēva - e. of Śrī Kṛṣṇa
विकास	Vikāsa - progress
विक्रम	Vikrama - courageous
विक्रमादित्य	Vikramāditya - radiant and courageous
विक्रान्त	Vikrānta - brave, victorious
विजय	Vijaya - victory
विट्ठल	Viṭṭhala - e. of Viṣṇu or Śrī Kṛṣṇa
विदुर	Vidura - wise, learned
विद्यानिवास	Vidyānivāsa - abode of knowledge
विद्यासागर	Vidyāsāgara - ocean of knowledge
विनम्र	Vinamra - gentle
विनय	Vinaya - modest
विनायक	Vināyaka - remover of obstacles - e. of Gaṇapati
विनीत	Vinīta - modest

विनोद	Vinōda - mirth
विपुल	Vipula - abundant
विभव	Vibhava - power, glory
विभु	Vibhu - all pervading, eternal
विमल	Vimala - pure
विमल कीर्ति	Vimala Kīrti - spotless fame
विवेक	Vivēka - discrimination
विशाल	Viśāla - great, extensive
विश्वजित	Viśvajita - conqueror of the world
विश्वनाथ	Viśvanātha - lord of the universe - e. of Śiva
विश्वम्भर	Viśvambhara - all sustaining, Supreme Lord
विश्वेश्वर	Viśvēśvara - lord of the universe, e. of Śiva
विश्वामित्र	Viśvāmitra - friend of all, n. of a ṛṣi
विष्णु	Viṣṇu - n. of God as protector and preserver
विष्णु दत्त	Viṣṇu Datta - gift of Viṣṇu
विष्णु नारायण	Viṣṇu Nārāyaṇa - Lord Viṣṇu
विष्णु प्रसाद	Viṣṇu Prasāda - grace of Viṣṇu
वीरेन्द्र	Vīrēndra - chief of the brave people
वेङ्कटेश/ वेङ्कटेश्वर	Vēṅkaṭēśa/Vēṅkaṭēśvara - Lord who resides on Vēnkat Hill - e. of Viṣṇu
वेदप्रकाश	Vēdaprakāśa - light of learning
वैभव	Vaibhava - glory
शङ्कर	Śaṅkara - beneficent, e. of Śiva
शतानन्द	Śatānanda - very happy person
शत्रुघ्न	Śatrughna - destroyer of enemy
शन्तनु	Śantanu - beneficent
शम्भु	Śambhu - beneficent - e. of Śiva
शम्भुनाथ	Śambhunātha - Lord Śiva
शरच्चन्द्र	Śaraccandra - autumnal moon
शशाङ्क	Śaśāṅka - moon
शशि	Śaśi - moon
शशिकान्त	Śaśikānta - moonstone, luster of moon
शशिभूषण	Śaśibhūṣaṇa - e. of Śiva

शान्ति देव	Śānti Dēva - peace granting lord
शालीन	Śālīna - modest
शिव	Śiva - auspicious, gracious, God
- दत्त	- datta - gift of Śiva
- दयाल	- dayāla - merciful Śiva
- दास	- dāsa - servant of Śiva
- नाथ	- nātha - Lord Śiva
- प्रसाद	- prasāda - grace of Śiva
- प्रकाश	- prakāśa - glory of Śiva
- प्रताप	- pratāpa - power of Śiva
- मूर्ति	- mūrtị - image of Śiva
शिवानन्द	Śivānanda - bliss of Śiva
शीलनिधि	Śīlanidhi - treasure of virtue
शुकदेव	Śukadēva - n. of s. of Vyāsa
शेखर	Śēkhara - crown, top
शैलेन्द्र/शैलेश	Śailēndra/Śailēśa - chief of mountains - Himālaya
शोभित	Śōbhita - splendid
श्याम सुन्दर	Śyāma Sundara - dark and handsome, e. of Śrī Kṛṣṇa
श्रीकान्त	Śrīkānta - beloved of Lakṣmī - Viṣṇu
श्रीधर	Śrīdhara - bearer of Lakṣmī, e. of Viṣṇu
श्रीनाथ	Śrīnātha - lord of Lakṣmī - Viṣṇu
श्रीनिवास	Śrīnivāsa - e. of Viṣṇu
श्रेयान्	Śrēyān - excellent
श्वेतांशु	Śvētāṃśu - white rayed-moon
सङ्कल्प	Saṅkalpa - determination
सच्चिदानन्द	Saccidānanda - bliss of absorption in Reality
सञ्जय	Sañjaya - victorious
सञ्जीव	Sañjīva - living a good life
सत्कृत	Satkṛta - worshipped, honored
सतीश	Satīśa - lord of Satī - e. of Śiva
सत्यकाम	Satyakāma - truth-lover
सत्यजित	Satyajita - truly victorious
सत्यनारायण	Satyanārāyaṇa - e. of Viṣṇu

सत्यव्रत Satyavrata - dedicated to truth
सत्येन्द्र Satyēndra - best among honest men
सदानन्द Sadānanda - perpetual bliss
सन्तोष Santōṣa - satisfaction
सन्दीप Sandīpa - to glow
समीर Samīra - wind
सर्वजित Sarvajita - conqueror of all
सर्वानन्द Sarvānanda - making all happy
सर्वेश/सर्वेश्वर Sarvēśa/Sarvēśvara - lord of all
सर्वोत्तम Sarvōttama - the best
सलिल Salila - flowing, water
सव्यसाची Savyasācī - able to aim with left hand - e. of Arjuna
सहदेव Sahadēva - with angels
सागर Sāgara - ocean
सारङ्ग Sāraṅga - peacock, Indian cuckoo, lotus, Śiva
सितांशु Sitāṃśu - moon
सिद्धार्थ Siddhārtha - successful in achieving his aim, n. of Buddha
सिद्धेश्वर Siddhēśvara - lord of the enlightened, Śiva
सुकुमार Sukumāra - handsome youth
सुकीर्ति Sukīrti - glorious
सुदर्शन Sudarśana - handsome
सुदीप Sudīpa - lustrous
सुद्युम्न Sudyumna - n. of s. of Manu Vaivasvata
सुधांशु Sudhāṃśu - moon
सुधाकर Sudhākara - moon
सुधीन्द्र Sudhīndra - excellent among bright men
सुधीर Sudhīra - very firm
सुनीत Sunīta - of good conduct, prudent
सुप्रतीक Supratīka - handsome
सुप्रभात Suprabhāta - beautiful dawn
सुबल Subala - mighty, e. of Śiva
सुबोध Subōdha - very learned

सुभाष	Subhāṣa - soft-spoken
सुभास	Subhāsa - lustrous
सुमति	Sumati - of good mind
सुमित	Sumita - well-built
सुयश	Suyaśa - of good repute
सुरेन्द्र/सुरेश	Surēndra/Surēśa - chief of gods, e. of Indra
सुव्रत	Suvrata - of good character
सुशान्त	Suśānta - very calm
सुशील	Suśīla - of good character
सुश्रुत	Suśruta - very famous
सुस्मित	Susmita - one with a smile
सुहास	Suhāsa - having a pleasant smile
सुहृद	Suhṛda - kind-hearted
सूर्यप्रकाश	Sūryaprakāśa - light of sun
सोमकान्त	Sōmakānta - lovely as moon
सोमदत्त	Sōmadatta - gift of moon
सोमेश/सोमेश्वर	Sōmēśa/Sōmēśvara - e. of moon
सौमित्र	Saumitra - son of Sumitrā - Lakṣmaṇa
सौम्य	Saumya - gentle
सौरभ	Saurabha - fragrance
स्कन्द	Skanda - e. of Kārttikēya
स्वर्णाभ	Svarṇābha - golden luster
हनुमान्	Hanumān - n. of a great devotee of Śrī Rāma
हरि ओम्	Hari Ōm - God is truth
हरि	Hari - Viṣṇu
- दत्त	- Datta - gift of Viṣṇu
- दयाल	- Dayāla - merciful Viṣṇu
- दास	- Dāsa - servant of Viṣṇu
- देव	- Dēva - Lord Viṣṇu
- प्रसाद	- Prasāda - grace of Viṣṇu
- मोहन	- Mōhana - charming Viṣṇu
- स्वरूप	- Svarūpa - image of Viṣṇu
हरिश्चन्द्र	Hariścandra - of golden splendor

हरीश	Harīśa - e. of Viṣṇu
हर्ष	Harṣa - delight
हितेश्वर	Hitēśvara - god of welfare
हिमांशु	Himāṃśu - moon
हेतल	Hētala - affectionate (Gujarātī)
हेमकान्त	Hēmakānta - golden luster
हेमन्त	Hēmanta - winter
हेरम्ब	Hēramba - e. of Gaṇapati

Recommended Middle Names for Boys

It is suggested that the names of boys consist of three words - first name, middle name, and last name. The most popular middle names are:

Traditional

कान्त	Kānta - handsome
कुमार	Kumāra - young prince
किशोर	Kiśōra - young man
चन्द्र	Candra - moon
दत्त	Datta - gift of
दयाल	Dayāla - kind
दास	Dāsa - servant
देव	Dēva - angel
नन्दन	Nandana - son, happy
नाथ	Nātha - master, master of
नारायण	Nārāyaṇa - Viṣṇu or Kṛṣṇa
निवास	Nivāsa - abode of
पाल	Pāla - protector
प्रकाश	Prakāśa - light
प्रसाद	Prasāda - grace of
मूर्ति	Mūrti - image
मोहन	Mōhana - attractive

सागर	Sāgara - ocean
सिंह	Siṃha - lion
सेन	Sēna - dependent on, body
स्वरूप	Svarūpa - form

Modern

आलोक	Ālōka - light
कमल	kamala - lotus
कल्याण	Kalyāṇa - wellbeing
गोविन्द	Gōvinda - e. of Śrī Kṛṣṇa
गौरव	Gaurava - glory
तिलक	Tilaka - in the forefront
ध्रुव	Dhruv - firm
नमित	Namita - humble
नलिन	Nalina - lotus
पीयूष	Pīyūṣa - nectar
प्रताप	Pratāpa - power, glory
प्रदीप	Pradīpa - lamp
प्रवीण	Pravīṇa - deft
प्रशान्त	Praśānta - calm
मणि	Maṇi - gem
मित्र	Mitra - friend
विकास	Vikāsa - growth
विनय	Vinaya - prayer
विपुल	Vipula - abundant
विमल	Vimala - pure
वीर	Vīra - brave
वैभव	Vaibhava - glory, fame
सिंह	Siṃha - lion

Note - that the correct English spelling of सिंह is Siṃha and not Singh, Singha, or Sinha as many people do. These would be सिंग, सिंघ, and सिन्हा respectively.

सुप्रिय	Supriya - very dear
सौरभ	Saurabha - fragrance

Types of Names of Boys to be Avoided

There can be no comprehensive list of names which should be avoided in future because it is impossible to collect and examine all the names of Hindū men in the world.

However, all the undesirable names can be divided into three categories: (1) with no meaning; (2) with undesirable meaning; and (3) corrupt forms.

The following list gives some of the names of all three categories.

Meaningless Names

अरुल - Arul
चीनू - Chinu
जेसल - Jesal
प्रेवेश - Prevesh
मुकेश - Mukesh
राजू - Raju
सेजल - Sejal

Names with Undesirable Meaning

अतीत	Atīta - past
अनिकेत	Anikēta - homeless
धीरेश	Dhīrēśa - master of the resolute
निमिष	Nimiṣa - wink
मितेश	Mitēśa - lord of very little
प्रतीक	Pratīka - inverted, symbol

Corrupt forms

चिमन	Cimana - corrupt of Chyavan (Cyavana)
मनहर	Manahara - corrupt of Manohar

Names for Girls

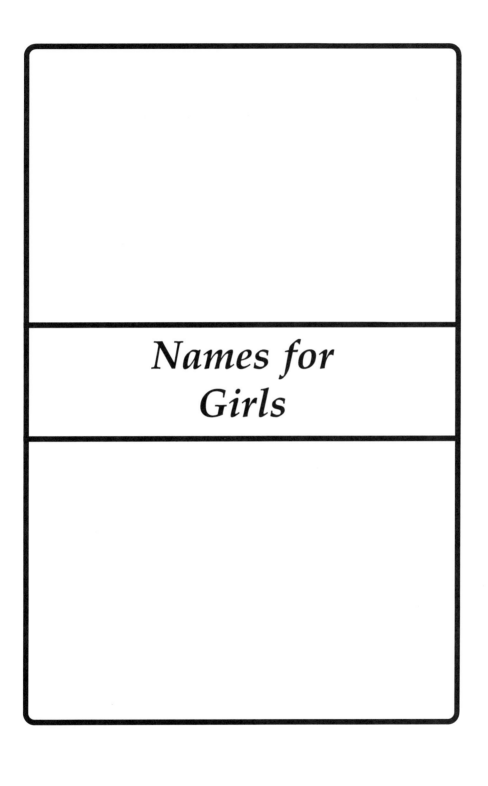

Recommended First Names for Girls

अंशुमाला	Aṃśumālā - garland of sun-rays
अकल्पिता	Akalpitā - unimaginable
अक्षमाला	Akṣamālā - rosary
अग्रिमा	Agrimā - in the forefront
अचला	Acalā - the earth, firm
अचिन्त्या	Acintyā - beyond imagination
अजेया	Ajēyā - undefeatable
अञ्जना	Añjanā - collyrium
अञ्जलि	Añjali - the hollow of joined palms
अञ्जु	Añju - (a meaningless word)
अतिभा	Atibhā - radiant
अतिरूपा	Atirūpā - very beautiful
अदिति	Aditi - infinity, n. of the mother of Ādityas
अनसूया	Anasūyā - not spiteful, n. of w. of ṛṣi Atri
अनामिका	Anāmikā - ring finger, nameless
अनिन्दिता	Aninditā - blameless
अनुपमा	Anupamā - matchless
अनुमोदिता	Anumōditā - delighted
अनुरञ्जिता	Anurañjitā - happy
अनुराधा	Anurādhā - n. of the 17th nakṣatra
अन्तरा	Antarā - in between, space
अन्नपूर्णा	Annapūrṇā - e. of Durgā, the provider of food
अपराजिता	Aparājitā - undefeatable
अपर्णा	Aparṇā - e. of Pārvatī
अपाला	Apālā - n. of a woman ṛṣi
अपूर्वा	Apūrvā - unprecedented
अमला	Amalā - stainless
अमिता	Amitā - immeasurable
अमिताभा	Amitābhā - of immeasurable splendor
अमृता	Amṛtā - immortal
अम्बा	Ambā - mother, e. of Durgā

अम्बालिका	Ambālikā - mother, e. of Durgā
अम्‌बिका	Ambikā - mother, e. of Durgā
अम्बुजा	Ambujā - lotus
अम्बुजाक्षी	Ambujākṣī - lotus-eyed
अरुजा	Arujā - healthy
अरुणा	Aruṇā - redness of dawn
अरुन्धती	Arundhatī - n. of the morning star
अर्‌चना	Arcanā - praise, worship
अर्‌चिता	Arcitā - praised
अर्‌पणा	Arpaṇā - offer
अर्‌पिता	Arpitā - offered
अलका	Alakā - n. of the capital of Kubēra
अल्का	Alkā - (mis-spelling of Alakā)
अवनी	Avanī - the earth
अवन्‌तिका	Avantikā - old n. of Ujjayinī city
आकाङ्‌क्षा	Ākāṅkṣā - desire
आद्‌या	Ādyā - excellent, e. of Durgā
आनन्दरूपा	Ānandarūpā - blissful
आनन्दी	Ānandī - e. of Gaurī
आभा	Ābhā - splendor
आराधना	Ārādhanā - worship
आशा	Āśā - hope
आस्था	Āsthā - confidence, faith
इन्‌दिरा	Indirā - e. of Lakṣmī
इन्दुकला	Indukalā - a digit of moon
इन्दुकान्ता	Indukāntā - splendor of moon
इन्दुप्रभा	Induprabhā - radiance of moon
इन्दुभा	Indubhā - light of moon
इन्दुमती	Indumatī - of full moon
इन्दुमुखी	Indumukhī - moon-faced
इन्द्राणी	Indrāṇī - Indra's wife
इरा	Irā - see Ilā
इरावती	Irāvatī - n. of a river

इला Ilā - n. of prototype of Sarasvatī
इशिता Iśitā - fast, speedy
ईशा Īśā - power
ईशिता Īśitā - supremacy
उज्ज्वला Ujjvalā - bright
उत्कर्षा Utkarṣā - superior
उत्कर्षिता Utkarṣitā - elevated
उत्कृष्टा Utkṛṣṭā - excellent
उत्तमा Uttamā - excellent
उत्तरा Uttarā - superior, higher
उत्पला Utpalā - blossom of water-lily
उदिता Uditā - elevated, risen
उपासना Upāsanā - worship
उमा Umā - n. of Śiva's w.
उर्मिला Urmilā - n. of w. of Lakṣmaṇa
उर्वशी Urvaśī - pervasive, n. of the most beautiful apsaras (heavenly nymph)
उशिजा Uśijā - desirable, charming
उषा Uṣā - dawn, goddess of dawn
ऊर्जा Ūrjā - energy
ऊर्जिता Ūrjitā - very energetic
ऋचा Ṛcā - praise, a mantra from the Vēdas
ऋजुता Ṛjutā - simplicity, honesty
ऋतम्भरा Ṛtambharā - true knowledge
ऋता Ṛtā - able, virtuous
ऋतावरी Ṛtāvarī - proper, truthful
ऋद्धि Ṛddhi - prosperity, good fortune
ऋषिका Ṛṣikā - woman ṛṣi
एधा Ēdhā - prosperity
एला Ēlā - cardamom, n. of a metre
ऐश्वरी Aiśvarī - e. of Durgā
कनक प्रभा Kanaka Prabhā - splendor of gold
कनक लता Kanaka Latā - golden creeper

कपिला	Kapilā - brown cow
कमला	Kamalā - e. of Lakṣmī
कमलाक्षी	Kamalākṣī - lotus-eyed
करुणा	Karuṇā - compassion
कर्णिका	Karṇikā - pericarp of lotus
कलावती	Kalāvatī - skilled and dexterous
कलिका	Kalikā - a small bud
कल्पना	Kalpanā - imagination, composition
कल्पलता	Kalpalatā - n. of a mythical creeper granting all desires
कल्याणी	Kalyāṇī - auspicious, e. of Pārvatī
कविता	Kavitā - poetry, poem
काजल	Kājala - colliriyum (Hindī)
काञ्चना (नी)	Kāñcanā (nī) - golden
कादम्बरी	Kādambarī - Indian female cuckoo, wine
कान्ता	Kāntā - beautiful woman
कान्तिमती	Kāntimatī - beautiful woman
कामना	Kāmanā - desire
कामाक्षी	Kāmākṣī - e. of Durgā
कामिनी	Kāminī - loving woman
काम्या	Kāmyā - beautiful, amiable
कार्त्तिकी	Kārttikī - Karttika pūrṇimā
कालिन्दी	Kālindī - another name of R. Yamunā
कावेरी	Kāvērī - n. of a river
किशोरी	Kiśōrī - young woman
किरणप्रभा	Kiraṇaprabhā - beam of light
कीर्तिमती	Kīrtimatī - glorious
कुन्ती	Kuntī - n. of a wife of K. Pāṇḍu
कुमुद	Kumuda - white water-lilly
कुमद्-वती	Kumad-vatī - bunch of water-lilys
कुसुम	Kusuma - flower
कुसुमकली	Kusumakalī - flower-bud
कुसुमाञ्जलि	Kusumāñjali - an offering of flowers inside joined palms
कुसुमिता	Kusumitā - blossom

कृति	Kṛti - original writing, production
कृत्तिका	Kṛttikā - n. of a nakṣatra
कृष्णा	Kṛṣṇā - real n. of Draupadī
केतकी	Kētakī - Pandanus (kēvrā) plant
कोकिला	Kōkilā - Indian cuckoo
कोमल	Kōmala - delicate, sweet
कौमुदी	Kaumudī - moon-light, festival
कौसल्या	Kausalyā - n. of the mother of Śrī Rāma
क्षमा	Kṣamā - forgiving
ख्याति	Khyāti - of good repute
गङ्गा	Gaṅgā - n. of the holiest river of Hindūs
गरिमा	Garimā - greatness, dignity
गायत्री	Gāyatrī - n. of the meter in which the famous Śavitrī mantra of Ṛgvēda has been composed. Because of this reason it is also called Gāyatrī mantra.
गार्गी	Gārgī - n. of a woman sage
गिरिजा	Girijā - d. of Himālaya - e. of Durgā
गिरीशा	Girīśā - e. of Durgā
गीता	Gītā - sacred song, short for Bhagavad-Gītā
गीताञ्जलि	Gītāñjali - a handful of songs
गीतिका	Gītikā - a short song
गुणवती	Guṇavatī - woman of talents
गौतमी	Gautamī - female descendant of Gotama
गौरी	Gaurī - white complexioned, e. of Durgā
घोषा	Ghōṣā - n. of a woman ṛṣi
चन्द्रकला	Candrakalā - a digit of moon's disc
चन्द्रकान्ता	Candrakāntā - w. of moon
चन्द्रप्रभा	Candraprabhā - moon-light
चन्द्रबाला	Candrabālā - d. of moon
चन्द्रमुखी	Candramukhī - moon-faced
चन्द्रलेखा	Candralēkhā - a digit of moon's disc
चन्द्रिका	Candrikā - moon-light
चपला	Capalā - lightning, e. of Lakṣmī

चम्पा	Campā - n. of a flower
चम्पावती	Campāvatī - a bunch of Campā flowers
चारुश्री	Cāruśrī - beautiful and graceful
चारुलता	Cārulatā - beautiful creeper
चार्वी	Cārvī - beautiful woman, moon-light
चित्रलेखा	Citralēkhā - picture, n. of a meter
चित्रा	Citrā - n. of an asterism
चित्राङ्गदा	Citrāṅgadā - picture-perfect beauty
चेतना	Cētanā - consciousness, intelligence
चैत्री	Caitrī - Caitra Pūrṇimā
छवि	Chavi - beauty, splendor
छान्दसी	Chāndasī - learned in the Vēdas
छाया	Chāyā - splendor, light, shadow
जगती	Jagatī - earth
जगदम्बा	Jagadambā - mother of the world, e. of Durgā
जगदम्बिका	Jagadambikā - see Jagadambā
जयलक्ष्मी	Jayalakṣmī - glory to Laksmī
जयश्री	Jayaśrī - see JayaLakṣmī
जयन्ती	Jayantī - victorious
जया	Jayā - victorious
जयित्री	Jayitrī - victorious
जानकी	Jānakī - d. of Janaka - e. of Sītā
जाह्नवी	Jāhnavī - d. of Jahnu - e. of R. Gaṅgā
जिगीषा	Jigīṣā - desirous of gaining or conquering
ज्योतिर्मयी	Jyōtirmayī - lustrous
ज्योत्स्ना	Jyōtsnā - moon-light
तनुश्री	Tanuśrī - divine body, lustrous body
तन्वी	Tanvī - delicate
तरङ्गिणी	Taraṅgiṇī - river
तारणी	Tāraṇī - enabling to cross over
तारा	Tārā - star
तुलसी	Tulasī - sacred basil plant
तूलिका	Tūlikā - painter's brush

तृप्ता (तृप्ति)	Tṛptā (Tṛpti) - satisfied
दक्षा	Dakṣā - dexterous
दमयन्ती	Damayantī - n. of w. of Nala
दया	Dayā - mercy
दाक्षायणी	Dākṣāyaṇī - e. of Durgā
दामिनी	Dāminī - lightning
दिव्या	Divyā - divine
दिशा	Diśā - direction
दीक्षा	Dīkṣā - initiation
दीपमाला	Dīpamālā - garland of lights
दीपशिखा	Dīpaśikhā - flame of a lamp
दीपा	Dīpā - illuminating
दीपाली	Dīpālī - a row of lights
दीपिका	Dīpikā - see Dīpā
दीप्ता (दीप्ति)	Dīptā (Dīpti) - brightness, beauty
दुर्गा	Durgā - n. of w. of Śiva
देवकी	Dēvakī - n. of m. of Śrī Kṛṣṇa
देवयानी	Dēvayānī - n. of a w. of K. Yayāti
देविका	Dēvikā - divine grace
देवी	Dēvī - goddess
द्रौपदी	Draupadī - a d. of K. Drupada, patronymic of Kṛṣṇā
द्युतिमती	Dyutimatī - radiant woman
धृतिमती	Dhṛtimatī - woman of firm resolve
नन्दा	Nandā - happiness
नन्दिता	Nanditā - happiness, one who makes others happy
नमिता	Namitā - modest
नम्रता	Namratā - modesty
नलिनी	Nalinī - lotus, bunch of water-lily flowers
नारायणी	Nārāyaṇī - e. of Lakṣmī or Durgā
नित्या	Nityā - eternal
निधि	Nidhi - wealth
निरञ्जना	Nirañjanā - pure
निरुपमा	Nirupamā - matchless

निर्मला	Nirmalā - clean, pure
निवेदिता	Nivēditā - offering, present
निशा	Niśā - night
निष्ठा	Niṣṭhā - faith, devotion
नीता	Nītā - well-mannered
नीतिपूर्णा	Nītipūrṇā - of wise or good conduct
नीरजा	Nīrajā - lotus, water-lily
नीलम	Nīlama - sapphire
नीलिमा	Nīlimā - blue, dark
नेहा	Nēhā - corrupt of Snehā meaning affectionate
पङ्कजा	Paṅkajā - lotus
पद्मा	Padmā - e. of Lakṣmī
पद्मावती	Padmāvatī - bunch of lotuses
पद्मिनी	Padminī - bunch of lotuses
पल्लवी	Pallavī - a young shoot
पार्वती	Pārvatī - e. of Durgā
पुष्पलता	Puṣpalatā - a creeper full of flowers
पुष्पा	Puṣpā - flower-like
पुष्पाञ्जलि	Puṣpāñjali - hollow of joined palms with flowers to offer to God or some one honored
पूजा	Pūjā - worship
पूर्णिमा	Pūrṇimā - night (and day) of full moon
पृथा	Pṛthā - another name of Kuntī, the w. of Pāṇḍu
प्रज्ञावती	Prajñāvatī - intelligent woman
प्रतिभा	Pratibhā - talent
प्रतिमा	Pratimā - image
प्रभा	Prabhā - light
प्रमुदिता	Pramuditā - happy
प्रमोदिनी	Pramōdinī - delighting
प्रशस्ति	Praśasti - praise
प्रशान्ता	Praśāntā - calm
प्रसन्ना	Prasannā - happy
प्रार्थना	Prārthanā - prayer

प्रियङ्का	Priyaṅkā - agreeable, kind
प्रियंवदा	Priyaṃvadā - soft-spoken
प्रियदर्शिनी	Priyadarśinī - pleasant to sight
प्रिया	Priyā - darling
प्रीता	Prītā - affectionate
प्रेमा	Prēmā - loving
फाल्गुनी	Phālgunī - n. of a nakṣatra, full moon day in Phālguna month
बाला	Bālā - girl
बृजबाला	Bṛjabālā - girl from Bṛja region, gopī
बेला	Bēlā - a flower of jasmine family
भगवती	Bhagavatī - e. of Lakṣmī
भागीरथी	Bhāgīrathī - d. of Bhagīratha, e. of R. Gaṅgā
भाग्यश्री	Bhāgyaśrī - goddess of fortune, e. of Lakṣmī
भामिनी	Bhāminī - beautiful woman
भारती	Bhāratī - Vedic n. of Lakṣmī
भावना	Bhāvanā - feeling of devotion, imagination
मङ्गला	Maṅgalā - auspicious
मञ्जरी	Mañjarī - cluster of blossoms
मञ्जु	Mañju - beautiful
मञ्जुला	Mañjulā - charming
मञ्जुलिका	Mañjulikā - beautiful
मञ्जुश्री	Mañjuśrī - divine beauty, e. of Lakṣmī
मणिप्रभा	Maṇiprabhā - splendor of a gem
मधुबाला	Madhubālā - sweet girl
मधुमती	Madhumatī - sweet girl
मधुरिमा	Madhurimā - sweetness
मधुलिका	Madhulikā - sweetness
मधुस्मिता	Madhusmitā - having a sweet smile
मनीषा	Manīṣā - wisdom
मनोरमा	Manōramā - charming, pleasing
मन्दाकिनी	Mandākinī - e. of R. Gaṅgā
ममता	Mamatā - motherly love

मल्लिका	Mallikā - a variety of Camēlī (jasmine) flower
महाश्वेता	Mahāśvētā - fair-complexioned
महिमा	Mahimā - glory
माधवी	Mādhavī - earth, spring flower
माधुरी	Mādhurī - loveliness
मानसी	Mānasī - mental, spiritual
मान्या	Mānyā - honorable
माया	Māyā - wealth, creation
मालती	Mālatī - a variety of jasmine flower
मालविका	Mālavikā - n. of the heroine in Mālavikāgnimitra drama by Kālidāsa
माला	Mālā - garland
मालिनी	Mālinī - woman who sells garlands and flowers
मीना	Mīnā - fish
मीनाक्षी	Mīnākṣī - woman with beautiful eyes
मीरा	Mīrā - n. of the famous poetess and devotee
मुकुलिता	Mukulitā - full of blossoms
मुक्ता	Muktā - pearl
मुदिता	Muditā - happy
मृणालिनी	Mṛṇālinī - lotus plant
मृदुला	Mṛdulā - tender
मेघना	Mēghanā - n. of a river
मेधा	Mēdhā - wisdom
मेनका	Mēnakā - n. of a heavenly nymph (apsaras)
मोहिता	Mōhitā - in love
मोहिनी	Mōhinī - one who attracts
यशस्विनी	Yaśasvinī - glorious
यशोदा	Yaśōdā - n. of foster m. of Śrī Kṛṣṇa
यशोधरा	Yaśōdharā - glorious, n. of w. of Gautama Buddha
यशोमती	Yaśōmatī - glorious woman, another name of Yaśodā
यामिनी	Yāminī - night
योगनिद्रा	Yōganidrā - meditative sleep, e. of Durgā
योगेश्वरी	Yōgēśvarī - adept in yōga, e. of Durgā

रक्षा	Rakṣā - protection
रचना	Racanā - composition, creation of something
रजनी	Rajanī - night
रञ्जना	Rañjanā - delighting
रञ्जिता	Rañjitā - delighted
रत्ना	Ratnā - jewel
रत्नावली	Ratnāvalī - a bunch of jewels
रत्नप्रभा	Ratnaprabhā - luster of a gem
रमा	Ramā - good luck, e. of Lakṣmī
रम्भा	Rambhā - lovable, e. of Pārvatī
रम्या	Ramyā - delighting
रश्मि	Raśmi - ray of light
राका	Rākā - a night (and day) of Purṇimā
रागिनी	Rāginī - music, love
राजकुमारी	Rājakumārī - princess
राजलक्ष्मी	Rājalakṣmī - royal majesty
राजेश्वरी	Rājēśvarī - queen
राधा	Rādhā - prosperity, success, short n. of Rukmiṇī
राधिका	Rādhikā - a form of the name Rādhā
रामा	Rāmā - charming
रामेश्वरी	Rāmēśvarī - consort of Śrī Rāma
रीता	Rītā - short form of Ṛtāvarī
रुक्मिणी	Rukmiṇī - n. of the w. of Śrī Kṛṣṇa
रुचि	Ruci - beauty
रुचिता	Rucitā - lustrous
रुचिरा	Rucirā - charming, beautiful
रेखा	Rēkhā - line, outline
रेणुका	Rēṇukā - sand, pollen, powder
रेवती	Rēvatī - n. of fifth nakṣatra, n. of a musical rāga
रेवा	Rēvā - another n. of Rati
रोचना	Rōcanā - beautiful woman
रोहिणी	Rōhiṇī - rising, n. of the ninth nakṣatra, another name of cow of plently, Kāmadhēnu

रोहिता	Rōhitā - rainbow, radiant
लक्ष्मी	Lakṣmī - prosperity, good luck, goddess of prosperity
लज्जा	Lajjā - modesty
लता	Latā - creeper, delicate woman, string of pearls
लतिका	Latikā - a delicate creeper, a string of pearls
ललिता	Lalitā - charming, graceful, n. of Durgā
लाजवन्ती	Lājavantī - modest woman (this is a Hindi and not a Saṃskṛta word)
लीना	Līnā - devoted, absorbed
लीला	Līlā - charm, grace
लोपामुद्रा	Lōpāmudrā - n. of a woman ṛṣi
वत्सला	Vatsalā - affectionate
वनिता	Vanitā - dear woman
वन्दना	Vandanā - praise, worship
वन्दिता	Vanditā - praised, worshipped
वर्तिका	Vartikā - paint brush, wick of lamp
वर्षा	Varṣā - rain, rainy season
वल्लरी	Vallarī - creeper
वसुधा	Vasudhā - granter of wealth, e. of earth, e. of Lakṣmī
वसुन्धरा	Vasundharā - earth, the generous earth
वागीशा	Vāgīśā - goddess of speech - Sarasvatī
वाणी	Vāṇī - voice, speech
वासन्ती	Vāsantī - n. of a variety of jasmine
वासवदत्ता	Vāsavadattā - gifted by Indra
विजयलक्ष्मी	Vijayalakṣmī - goddess of victory
विजया	Vijayā - e. of Durgā
विजिता	Vijitā - victorious
विदिता	Viditā - knowledgeable, learned, famous
विदुषी	Viduṣī - wise woman, learned woman
विद्या	Vidyā - knowledge
विनीता	Vinītā - decent, modest
विनोदिनी	Vinōdinī - pleasing
विपुला	Vipulā - abundant, earth

विभा	Vibhā - light, beauty
विभूति	Vibhūti - great power, sacred ashes put on the forehead by devotees
विमला	Vimalā - clean, bright
विलक्षणा	Vilakṣaṇā - distinguished
विश्ववारा	Viśvavārā - n. of a woman ṛṣi
वीणा	Vīṇā - a sitar-type musical instrument with gourd on both sides
वृन्दा	Vṛndā - a name of Rādhā
वृन्देश्वरी	Vṛndēśvarī - goddess Lakṣmī
वेणी	Vēṇī - stream
वेला	Vēlā - limit
वैजयन्ती	Vaijayantī - garland of victory, garland of Viṣṇu
वैदेही	Vaidēhī - e. of Sītā
वैशाली	Vaiśālī - n. of kingdom est. by K. Viśāla
शङ्करी	Śaṅkarī - e. of Durgā
शकुन्तला	Śakuntalā - n. of the mother of K. Bharata
शची	Śacī - n. of w. of Indra
शर्मिष्ठा	Śarmiṣṭhā - fortunate, n. of a w. of K. Yayāti
शशिकला	Śaśikalā - a digit of moon
शशिप्रभा	Śaśiprabhā - moon-light
शान्ता	Śāntā - tranquil, calm
शान्ति	Śānti - peace, peaceful
शारदा	Śāradā - n. of Sarasvatī
शालिनी	Śālinī - amply provided
शिखा	Śikhā - peak, flame
शिक्षा	Śikṣā - education
शिप्रा	Śiprā - n. of a holy river
शिल्पा	Śilpā - artist
शिवानी	Śivānī - Śiva's w. - Durgā
शीला	Śīlā - virtuous woman
शुभलक्ष्मी	Śubhalakṣmī - propitious goddess Lakṣmī
शुभा	Śubhā - auspicious

शुभाङ्गी	Śubhāṅgī - beautiful-limbed
शुभ्रा	Śubhrā - bright, fair-complexioned
शेफाली	Śēphālī - fragrant, Harsiṅgār flower
शेफालिका	Śēphālikā - see Shephālī
शैलजा	Śailajā - d. of mountain - Pārvatī
शैला	Śailā - e. of Pārvatī
शैली	Śailī - style
शैवी	Śaivī - auspicious
शोभना	Śōbhanā - beautiful, virtuous
शोभा	Śōbhā - beauty
शोभिता	Śōbhitā - adorned
श्यामला	Śyāmalā - a name for Durgā
श्यामा	Śyāmā - a name for Durgā
श्रद्‌धा	Śraddhā - faith, confidence
श्रावणी	Śrāvaṇī - Śrāvaṇa Pūrṇimā
श्रिया	Śriyā - prosperity
श्रीदेवी	Śrīdēvī - Lakṣmī, the goddess of prosperity
श्रीलता	Śrīlatā - divine creeper
श्वेता	Śvētā - fair-complexioned
सङ्गीता	Saṅgītā - symphony
सञ्जना	Sañjanā - affectionate
सती	Satī - virtuous, faithful to husband
सत्या	Satyā - truthful
सन्‌ध्या	Sandhyā - twilight of morning or evening, special prayer said at twilight
सप्ना	Sapnā - dream (corrupt of svapnā)
समीक्षा	Samīkṣā - investigation
सरला	Saralā - straight forward
सरस्वती	Sarasvatī - goddess of speech and wisdom
सरिता	Saritā - river
सरोजा	Sarōjā - water-lily
सरोजिनी	Sarōjinī - bunch of water-lilies
सर्‌वप्रिया	Sarvapriyā - dear to all

साधना	Sādhanā - action to accomplish
साध्वी	Sādhvī - righteous, saintly
सामन्ता	Sāmantā - neighbor
सारिका	Sārikā - confidante, mynā bird
सावित्री	Sāvitrī - sun, actual n. of a mantra popularly called Gāyatrī
सीता	Sītā - n. of w. of Śrī Rāma
सीमा	Sīmā - boundary, land-mark
सुकन्या	Sukanyā - good girl
सुकीर्ति	Sukīrti - praiseworthy
सुचित्रा	Sucitrā - famous
सुजाता	Sujātā - beautiful
सुदर्शना	Sudarśanā - good-looking woman
सुदीप्ता	Sudīptā - radiant woman
सुधा	Sudhā - nectar, earth
सुनन्दा	Sunandā - delighting
सुनयना	Sunayanā - woman with beautiful eyes
सुनीता	Sunītā - well-mannered, polite woman
सुन्दरी	Sundarī - beautiful woman
सुप्रिया	Supriyā - very dear
सुभगा	Subhagā - very fortunate
सुभद्रा	Subhadrā - very bright or fortunate, n. of w. of Arjuna
सुभाषिणी	Subhāṣiṇī - soft-spoken
सुमति	Sumati - of good mind
सुमनलता	Sumanalatā - a creeper full of flowers
सुमित्रा	Sumitrā - good friend, n. of mother of Lakṣmaṇa and Śatrughna
सुरभि	Surabhi - fragrance
सुरुचि	Suruci - radiant, delightful
सुलक्षणा	Sulakṣaṇā - fortunate, of great qualities
सुलभा	Sulabhā - attainable
सुलोचना	Sulōcanā - woman of beautiful eyes
सुवर्णा	Suvarṇā - woman of good complexion

सुशान्ता	Suśāntā - very calm
सुशीला	Suśīlā - good-tempered, virtuous
सुषमा	Suṣamā - exquisite beauty
सुस्मिता	Susmitā - woman with a beautiful smile
सुहासिनी	Suhāsinī - woman with a beautiful smile
सौम्या	Saumyā - gentle, pleasant
स्निग्धा	Snigdhā - affectionate, gentle
स्नेहलता	Snēhalatā - vine of affection
स्नेहा	Snēhā - affectionate
स्वर्णलता	Svarṇalatā - golden creeper
स्वस्तिमती	Svastimatī - fortunate
स्वाति	Svāti - n. of a nakṣatra
हरिणी	Hariṇī - female deer
हर्षना	Harṣanā - causing delight
हर्षा	Harṣā - happy
हर्षिता	Harṣitā - happy
हिमाद्रि	Himādri - e. of Pārvatī
हेमकान्ता	Hēmakāntā - bright as gold
हेमलता	Hēmalatā - golden creeper
हेमा	Hēmā - (short of Hemāṅgī)
हेमाङ्गी	Hēmāṅgī - woman with golden limbs
हेमामालिनी	Hēmāmālinī - woman with a golden garland

Middle Names of Girls

There is practically no tradition of middle names for Hindū girls. When the parents feel that a name seems somewhat inadequate they add a suffix which becomes a part of the first name of the girl. The following suffixes are common:

कुमारी	Kumārī - young girl, princess - for example Rājakumārī, Shivakumārī etc.;

देवी Dēvī - goddess - for ex. Lakshmīdevī, Durgādēvī etc.

मती Matī - edowed with - for example Indumatī, Kīrtimatī etc.;

वती Vatī - same as matī - for example Kalāvatī, Prabhāvatī, Drishadvati etc.;

श्री Śrī - grace - for example Chāruśrī, Jayaśrī etc.;

प्रभा Prabhā - radiance or splendor - for example Shashiprabhā, Chandraprabhā etc.

The suffixes matī and vatī are the same except in the case of words ending in a (अ) or ā (आ) sounds and consonants such as Kalā or Prabhā and Dṛṣad, vatī is used and in all other cases matī is used. Some people separate a suffix to make it look like the middle name, for example instead of Rājakumārī they will write Rāja Kumārī, or instead of writing Indumatī they will write Indu Matī and so on.

Types of Names of Girls to be Avoided

There can be no comprehensive list of names which have been used and which should be avoided in future unless every Hindu girl's name in the world has been known.

However, all the undesirable names can be divided into five categories: (1) with no meaning; (2) with undesirable meaning, (3) masculine names for girls, (4) corrupt forms, and (5) foreign names. The following list gives some of the names that are not very desirable.

Meaningless Names

अज्जु	Ajju	अनीता	Anītā
अञ्जु	Añju	अलीशा	Alīśā
कमलेश	Kamalēśa	किरणदीप	Kiraṇadīpa
जयना	Jayanā	निकी	Nikī
नीरू	Nīrū	नीना	Nīnā
प्रेमिला	Prēmilā	बीजल	Bījala
रीमा	Rīmā	रीमी	Rīmī
रूपल	Rūpala		

Names with Undesirable Meaning

अनीशा	Anīśā - helpless, without God
अल्पा	Alpā - little, trifling
तरला	Taralā - trembling
रेष्मा	Rēṣmā - whirlwind
शीना	Śīnā - frozen

Masculine Names

मिथिलेश	Mithilēśa - masculine without adding Kumārī

Corrupt Forms

अमी	Amī - corrupt of Amritā
निशी	Niśī - corrupt of Nishā meaning night
पूर्वी	Pūrvī - corrupt of Purvā meaning first
भाविका	Bhāvikā - corrupt of Bhavikī meaning existing

Foreign Names

करिश्मा	Kariśmā - (Persian)
नटाशा	Naṭāśā - (Russian)
तान्या	Tānyā - (Russian)
मोनिका	Mōnicā - (European)
मोना	Mōnā - (European)